Candletown
Can you find Puddle Lane?

USING THIS BOOK

*One of the best ways of helping children to learn to read is by reading stories to them and with them. This way they learn what **reading** is, and they will gradually come to recognise many words, and begin to read for themselves.*

First, grown-ups read the story on the left-hand pages aloud to the child.

You can reread the story as often as the child enjoys hearing it. Talk about the pictures as you go.

Later the child is encouraged to read the words under the pictures on the right-hand page.

The pages at the back of the book will give you some ideas for helping your child to read.

British Library Cataloguing in Publication Data
McCullagh, Sheila K.
    The wideawake mice find a new home. —
    (Puddle Lane)
    1. Readers — 1950-
    I. Title   II. Morris, Tony *(date)*
    III. Series
    428.6   PE1119
    ISBN 0-7214-0923-7

First edition

Published by Ladybird Books Ltd Loughborough Leicestershire UK
Ladybird Books Inc Lewiston Maine 04240 USA

Printed in England

The Wideawake Mice find a new home

written by SHEILA McCULLAGH
illustrated by TONY MORRIS

This book belongs to:

Ladybird Books

If you have not yet read Book 6, Stage 1,
The Wideawake Mice, *read this aloud first.*

The Wideawake Mice were toy mice,
in Mr Wideawake's toy shop.
One evening, the Magician
came into the shop.
He didn't see the Wideawake Mice,
but he spilt some magic dust
all over them.
That night, when the moon shone down,
the Wideawake Mice came alive.
They escaped from the shop
through a hole under the door, and
ran across the square to the market.
They climbed up a post and found
a safe place to live on a shelf
under the roof.

This is another story about their
adventures.

the Wideawake Mice

It was Friday evening.
Friday was market day in Candletown.
Every Friday, after the people
had gone home, the Wideawake Mice
went into the market.

The Wideawake Mice
went into the market.

They ate pieces of cheese and pieces
of cake. They ate nuts and
carrots and apples, until
Grandmother Mouse said,
"I can't eat another thing,"
and Grandfather Mouse said,
"It's time to go home."
He went to the post,
to climb up to the roof, and
the other mice followed him.

The Wideawake Mice
ate nuts and cheese.

The moon was just coming up
over the houses.
It shone on the market building.
Jeremy Mouse was just going
to climb up the post to the roof,
when he saw a big nut
lying on the floor.
"I must just get that nut,"
said Jeremy.

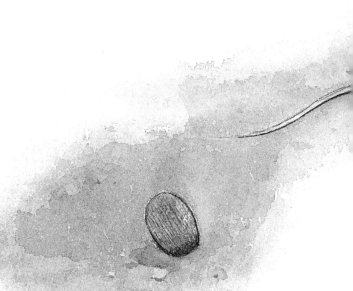

Jeremy saw a nut.

The other mice were all climbing the post.
Jeremy ran across to the nut.
He was just going to pick it up,
when a voice said,
"You leave that alone! That's mine!"
Jeremy looked up, and saw a big rat.
"Go away!" cried the rat.
"Go away, or I'll bite you!
And don't let me see you again."

Jeremy saw a rat.

"But I live here," said Jeremy.

"If I see you again,
you won't **live** here any longer,"
said the rat. "Go away, and
don't come back!"
Jeremy ran away. He ran back to the post.
He climbed up, and met Aunt Jane.
Aunt Jane was just coming
to look for him.

14

Jeremy ran away.
He met Aunt Jane.

"There's a big rat down there
in the market, Aunt Jane," cried Jeremy.
"He said that I couldn't live here
any longer. I think he meant
that he'd eat me!"
All the other mice crowded round
to listen.

"Oh dear! Oh dear!" said Aunt Matilda.
"Whatever shall we do?"

"We must go away,"
said Grandfather Mouse.
"Rats are very dangerous.
We must find somewhere else to live."

Grandfather Mouse
said,
''We must go away.''

"Let's go and live
in the Magician's garden," said Jeremy.
"I met a mouse the other day,
his name is Chestnut, and he lives
in a hollow tree in the garden."

"It sounds a good place,"
said Grandfather Mouse.
"But how do we get there?
We don't know the way."

"I do," said Miranda. "I've been there.
I saw the Magician.
The Magician's house is in Puddle Lane."

"Then you can show us the way,"
said Grandfather Mouse.
"We'll start at once."

Miranda said,
"I saw the Magician.
The Magician's house
is in Puddle Lane."

The mice were soon ready to go.
Miranda and Jeremy made their clothes
into bundles, and Aunt Jane helped them
to tie the bundles on their backs
with string.
Then they all ran down the post
to Market Square.

The Wideawake Mice
ran down the post.

They were just going to start out
across the square, when Uncle Maximus
said, "I smell cheese!"
He looked round a corner,
and saw the cheese.
There was a little bit of cheese
on a spike.
Uncle Maximus was just going to eat it,
when Aunt Jane called out,
"Don't touch it! It's a trap!"

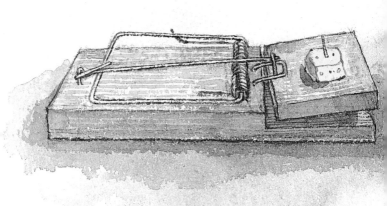

Uncle Maximus
saw the cheese.

Uncle Maximus jumped sideways,
but he was just too late.
The trap went snap!
It caught the end of his tail.
"Help!" cried Uncle Maximus. "Help!"

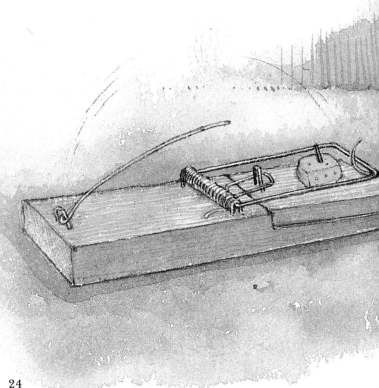

The trap went snap!

The other mice tried to pull
the trap open,
but it was much too strong.
They pulled and they pulled and
they PULLED, but
they couldn't pull up the wire.

The mice pulled,
and they pulled,
and they PULLED.

Aunt Jane took Grandfather's stick.
"We'll open it with this," she said.
She pushed the stick under the wire.
Grandfather pushed on one end
of the stick,
and Aunt Jane pushed on the other.
Miranda ran to help Grandfather push,
and Jeremy helped Aunt Jane.
They pushed and they pushed
and they PUSHED.

The mice pushed,
and they pushed,
and they PUSHED.

Slowly, very slowly,
the trap began to open.
"Pull out your tail!" cried Aunt Jane.
Uncle Maximus pulled out his tail.
The mice let go of the stick,
and the trap snapped to again.

Uncle Maximus
pulled out his tail.

"Oh, my poor tail!" cried Uncle Maximus.
"Oh, my poor tail!"

"Come along quickly,
and don't make a fuss,"
said Grandfather Mouse,
picking up his stick.
"We must go as fast as we can."

Miranda led the way across the square,
and all the other mice followed.
(Uncle Maximus carried his tail
over his arm.)

Miranda led the way.

They came to the corner of Puddle Lane.
Miranda led the way up the lane.
They hadn't gone far,
when they heard a great clatter.
The mice all hid in the shadows.
But it was only Mrs Pitter-Patter
shutting her window.
The Wideawake Mice ran on.

Mrs Pitter-Patter
shut her window.
The Wideawake Mice
ran on.

They hadn't gone far,
when they heard a great roar.
The mice all hid in the shadows.
But it was only Mr Puffle.
Mr Puffle was in bed.
He was fast asleep, and
he was beginning to snore.
The Wideawake Mice ran on.

Mr Puffle was in bed.
The Wideawake Mice
ran on.

They hadn't gone far, when they heard
a great bang.
The mice all hid in the shadows.
But it was only Mr Gotobed,
falling out of bed.
The Wideawake Mice ran on.

Mr Gotobed
fell out of bed.
The Wideawake Mice
ran on.

They came to the gates of
the Magician's garden.
There was Chestnut Mouse.
He was sitting under the gate,
eating a nut.
He was very glad to see them.

Chestnut Mouse

So the Wideawake Mice went to live
with Chestnut, in a hole under the
hollow tree, in the Magician's garden.
And while they stayed there,
they were all quite safe.

The Wideawake Mice
in the hole in the tree

Notes for the parent/teacher

Turn back to the beginning, and print the child's name in the space on the title page, using ordinary, not capital letters.

Now go through the book again. Look at each picture and talk about it. Point to the caption below, and read it aloud yourself.

Run your finger along under the words as you read, so that the child learns that reading goes from left to right.

Encourage the child to read the words under the illustrations. Don't rush in with the word before he/she has had time to think, but don't leave him/her struggling.

Read this story as often as the child likes hearing it. The more opportunities he/she has of looking at the illustrations and **reading** the captions with you, the more he/she will come to recognise the words.

If you have several books, let the child choose which story he/she would like.

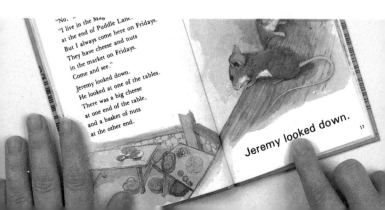